LET ZYGONS BE ZYGONS

Book Three of a trilogy of
autobiographical anecdotes
by Simon Fisher-Becker

LET ZYGONS BE ZYGONS

Book Three of a trilogy of autobiographical anecdotes by Simon Fisher-Becker

FIRST EDITION

First published by Fantastic Books Publishing 2021

ISBN (ebook): 978-1-914060-18-2

ISBN (paperback): 978-1-914060-17-5

Dedication

To my husband, Tony Dugdale

James Burgess, James and his Monsters

THE BOOK SOME
WANTED BANNED

Foreword by Joseph McGrail-Bateup

Joseph McGrail-Bateup

I had been a long-term Facebook friend with Simon Fisher-Becker through a mutual friend. It would be 5 years though before we actually spoke to each other.

Being a *Doctor Who* and Harry Potter fan I knew who Simon was. During Lockdown 2020, to relieve the boredom, Scott Radburn and I started The Joe & Scott Trivia Show. We asked Simon if he would like to be a guest. Based in Australia we weren't sure he would be interested. Simon said he would have to think about it. To our surprise within one second, he said yes – and what a contribution he made to the show.

This was the beginning of a truly special friendship. Simon arranged for Ian McNeice and Colin Spaull to come on the show and things developed from there.

Due to other commitments Scott had to leave the show. What was I going to do? I contacted Simon and asked if he'd like to be a co-host. To my amazement, he said YES straight away. He couldn't commit to every week, so this is how the newly titled *No-Name Trivia Show* came into existence with a second co-host – Paul Boultwood.

1

The show has grown with a following across the world, from Australia to the UK, France, Ireland and the United States. It didn't take Simon long to develop his own unique style and introduce a segment called Simon Says which is hugely successful. In addition, we all discovered how much work he has done which is extraordinary.

Having read *My Dalek Has A Puncture* and *My Dalek Has Another Puncture* I thought I knew a lot about Simon and respected how much he has achieved despite facing bullying and adversity in his early years. It's not until working with him I discovered his kindness, professionalism and clear determination to succeed. His flexibility to make something work and the sheer delight he has in helping others.

On occasions Simon has been criticised for being too political or controversial but if you've read his previous autobiographical anecdotes, you'll find *Let Zygons Be Zygons* a marvellous last part of a trilogy bringing us up to 2021; showing you what an insightful, inspiring and caring human being he really is.

Once international travel is allowed again my first trip will be to the UK to meet face to face this incredible fact-finder and storyteller. To Simon's many fans I promise you *Let Zygons Be Zygons* is a real page turner that will not disappoint. Somehow, I feel there will be a need for a fourth volume of the Trilogy!

Congrats Simon on this third book, may your fans enjoy the humour, grit, candid observations, and honesty as much as I have.

Lord Joseph McGrail-Bateup
Lord of Lochaber, Glencoe & Dunans Castle
The No-Name Trivia Show

Introduction

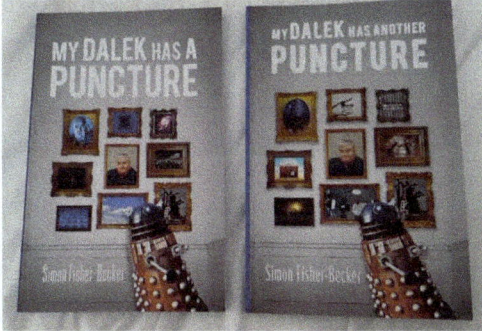

The response to my autobiographical anecdotes, *My Dalek Has A Puncture* and *My Dalek Has Another Puncture* has been wonderful, unexpected and at times overwhelming. I want to thank Dan Grubb and Fantastic Books Publishing for their continued support and naturally, you the reader, for your generous feedback. Your subsequent anecdotes and questions as well as concern for what's in store for the future show me my scribblings have hit a nerve and ignited the need to debate.

In this, the third of the trilogy, I hope *Let Zygons Be Zygons* will help address issues brought to my attention, answer your questions, and continue to help and motivate others.

2020 brought us a pandemic which meant taking extraordinary measures to get through it. Initially there was confusion and frustration which affected us all. This is not the forum to discuss the global and local political ramifications.

On a personal level, 2020 was emotional, frustrating, and highly stressful. My close family have been incredibly lucky. But many good friends have died of COVID-19. Not being able to go to their funerals was devastating and added to the loss.

Initially, in March 2020 my entire income stream came to a full stop. Sharp intake of breath and tightening of sphincter. In the UK, the

Government offered a self-employed support scheme. Hurrah, I cried with delight. Hope, wonderful. Relax. I then found, like millions of self-employed, that on a technicality I did not 'meet the criteria'.

So, no support scheme coming my way.

This news made me angry and bitter. My stubborn streak refused to believe the injustice of my plight. I first became self-employed in 1984 and over the years paid plenty into the system. To find that when I needed support because of a situation that was not of my making – let's just say I wasn't a happy puppy.

Tony, my husband, became self-employed in 2019 and was unable to provide three years of accounts as self-employed. He, therefore, wasn't entitled to any support either. In nearly 40 years I have never been in a position where no income of any kind was coming in. This was a very new and uncomfortable situation.

There were more than a few sleepless nights. The Government announced they would be giving money to banks to help customers. The only thing my bank offered was credit cards and loans. How could they expect anyone to pay loans off with no income?

Tony and I started to bicker – not intentionally. The situation brought a tension to our relationship which has never been there in 30 years.

One afternoon I had a real tantrum after speaking to yet another official telling me I simply didn't qualify for any support. Tony started to laugh; reminding me that when I throw a tantrum, I look like Winnie the Pooh.

I sat in my comfy chair in the living room and sulked. Whilst mulling things over and chewing wasps I heard my grandmother's voice, 'Take a deep breath and let bygones be bygones.'

Hence the title of this book with a *Doctor Who* twist.

The following day I woke up and said, 'If I can't pay a bill, I can't. If they choose to get stroppy about it – tell them, 'See you in court.'

Introduction

What to do with myself? I couldn't just sit in my chair or lie in bed all day.

Fantastic Books Publishing had commissioned *Let Zygons Be Zygons*. Steve Long, the producer for the audio sci-fi drama, *Hawk Chronicles* was still sending in new scripts and gradually other audio work came in. This helped keep my spirits up and structure my day.

In addition, I was invited by Christian Basel to be an occasional panellist on *The Legend of the Traveling Tardis* radio podcasts based in Orlando, Florida. Plus, Joseph McGrail-Bateup invited me to be a co-host on the popular *No-Name Trivia Show* based in Canberra, Australia. The extreme time differences have their own challenges but more of them later. Excellent, things to do!

Having read the first two volumes of this trilogy, you'll recall I often unwittingly court controversy. Word has got out that *Let Zygons Be Zygons* is my opportunity to 'name names'. There have been vailed threats of physical harm if I do. There are also some who have said they simply don't want to be mentioned.

Have I taken heed of the threats? That's for you, dear reader, to find out. I've suggested to Fantastic Books Publishing however, there should perhaps be a tag line: 'The book that some wanted banned'.

1

Where Do I Begin?

Where do I begin indeed …?

Having turned sixty, I reflect on what my grandmother once told me. 'In a funny way, things sort themselves out.' Being that much older, having experienced what life can throw at me, I understand and appreciate what she said. Things do sort themselves out either through intervention or by accident.

An example I repeat regularly is this; if I hadn't been attacked in March 2009, I wouldn't have been available to audition for *Doctor Who*. Being associated with *Doctor Who* changed my life completely.

There are so many variables. Sometimes I feel we shouldn't be bludgeoned into creating a fixed plan for our lives. When I was at school, in the 1970s, we were encouraged to build five-year plans. We should achieve certain goals every five years. A few of my class managed their five-year plan well but for the vast majority, life got in the way.

For some, the inability to achieve their goals within the given time frame added to the stresses of life, leading to feelings of inadequacy and low esteem. Some stuck to their ultimate goals and eventually achieved them. It may have taken much longer than they thought but en route, they built up different experiences and met a lot more people than they may have, had they stuck to a rigid path. Most say they feel good. Others feel lack of achievement held them back.

People can be cruel at times: Despite being a tolerant society, certain groups are extremely aggressive towards those they consider lazy wasters or scroungers, saying that they should 'pull themselves together'. There are many, alas, who believe there is no such thing as having wellbeing issues.

Within my family, I've witnessed first-hand the difficulties of living with mental health and wellbeing issues. At times I've felt inadequate. I was bullied at school by teachers and students. At the time, I was told I was either making up accusations or 'Never mind, move on, it's all character building.' Very frustrating. But it never crossed my mind NOT to go to school. I just put up with the daily abuse.

Part of my 'character building' is, as an adult, I spot bullying a mile off and am quick to come to the defence of victims, which at times gets me into trouble. I also have a profound distrust of those in authority. Some say it's because I'm an anarchist at heart. But that's because they're using the wrong term. Anarchism is to be sceptical of authority and call for the abolition of the State.

Yes, I'm suspicious of authority for good reason, but I'm certainly not against a simply structured State. I'll concede to being devil's advocate perhaps, or agent provocateur in the loosest of meanings.

Under no stretch of the imagination do I ever encourage people to break the law. I do, however, try to motivate people to think for themselves and avoid accepting everything carte blanche. If you feel you're being treated unjustly then assert that feeling with clear reasoning. When I've mentioned this before, some have felt it rash, leading only to trouble.

To clarify, consider this: many of you will have had the experience of being asked to get certain documents to certain offices by certain times. When I don't get an acknowledgement, I call the offices. The person I'm talking to is often disinterested and tries to fob me off with, 'We've not received it' or 'You didn't send it in on time.' What I've learned is this is part of a game. I go along with it, pretending to be confused. 'Oh, I'm sure I sent in, I can visualise myself posting it.'

The person is often very condescending and is about to end the call when I suddenly say, 'Oh I'm sorry, I forgot – I sent it in Recorded Delivery.' I then proceed to give the Recorded Delivery Number and the date posted – well before the due by date. There follows a long pause. I can hear the frantic tapping of keyboards. The person gets back to me, suddenly my documents are found. No apology!

Is this me being an anarchist or agent provocateur? Of course not. Assertive yes, after all I knew I had posted documents in good time. Many years ago, I would have shied away from being assertive, but this sort of thing has happened far too often. The wonderful feeling of getting something done by simply standing my ground became addictive, which in turn built my confidence. The secret is to be prepared and keep things simple.

Enter William of Ockham 1285 – 1347.

Born in the village of Ockham in Surrey (UK), William was a Franciscan friar, theologian and scholastic philosopher who is credited with developing a principle known as Occam's Razor.

If, when all the facts are considered for a specific situation and there are two or more plausible reasons put forward, the simpler one is probably nearer the truth.

When analysing the facts, you should gradually discard or cut away inconsistent facts before coming to final choices or conclusions. The act of cutting away these facts is where the term razor originates.

For example: You are walking around your garden. You notice a few broken fences. There are two possible explanations: a passing horse or cow has crashed into them, or a few nails have rusted away.

Both explanations seem reasonable, but you need more evidence. If you live in a rural area where there are stables and farm animals, a horse or cow crashing into the fences is more likely. But if you live in a city, it is more likely that nails have simply rusted away.

Critics of Occam's Razor say the principle doesn't work for more complex issues. That's up for debate. Personally, I think the principle can work for most situations. During the COVID-19 pandemic for example, the global effect has been devastating. The response from most, if not all, countries is to introduce measures such as furlough and other support schemes to avoid a global economic meltdown. The simplest of all options available. Occam's razor.

'Why have you taken this diversion?' I hear you cry. It's more a suggestion than a diversion. During lockdown I've had time to think and realise I've subconsciously practiced the principle of Occam's razor for many years before I discovered William Ockham.

Lockdowns have magnified issues for certain people. The main concern has been people's metal health. The term wellbeing is too flimsy and can disguise or dilute the true issue. In the UK, the first lockdown started March 2020. Initially, I enjoyed the novelty of it. The simple conditions set by the UK Government and scientists were not complicated.

Wash your hands regularly.

Wear a mask.

Only leave your house if you are an essential worker or need to take an essential journey to a doctor's surgery, a hospital or to go shopping.

If you go out, keep six feet apart from others – social distancing.

Being self-employed, both Tony and I bury ourselves in our offices at home most of the time anyway. We live in the country so the chances of bumping into crowds of people is limited. We quickly established the times when the supermarket was less busy. We tried home delivery for groceries but found the time slots were quickly taken. It didn't bother us. After all, the trip to the supermarket became the highlight of the week.

Apart from our initial financial situation everything was fine. We soon developed a routine. Thank you, dear fans. Receiving a regular flow of fan mail and being invited to take part in podcasts and Zoom meetings helped keep cabin fever at bay. Gradually some work came in but nowhere the amount I was used to. I also enjoyed the time I had to get on with my writing projects including *Let Zygons Be Zygons*. In the main I felt good.

The novelty wore off after a short while. I missed visiting my family and friends. Speaking to them online via WhatsApp or Facebook was fine. At least I could see them. But it's not the same as sitting in front of someone enjoying their company. I'm not sure if I got depressed about this situation but it was definitely frustrating.

Like so many others, I had good friends die of COVID-19. Mark Longman was the first. He was the organiser of Geek Events and booked me into most of them. Through Mark I discovered so much of the UK and joked I was a human SatNav. His events were always friendly and fun. Working with him and his fiancé, Jayne McMahon, such a joy. He was only 46 years old. His death hit home the reality of the pandemic. For those who bang on about conspiracy theories including 'COVID isn't real' – I despair!

Several other friends and associates died as well as my unofficial father-in-law, Allan Pearson. Not being able to get to their funerals was disturbing but having access via the internet was excellent. We had a scare with Tony, not Covid-related but an ambulance had to be called and he was taken to hospital. Being told I couldn't go with him was tough. Furthermore, we didn't get to say a proper goodbye. That was very tough and emotional. Fortunately, after six hours I was called, Tony was fine, I could collect him.

So, dear reader, I fully understand the heartache and pressures people are under and feel I'm qualified to answer questions. I never give advice; I merely make suggestions and it's up to you to run with them or not: Think for yourself and take responsibility for your actions.

Research shows that in society today most people are fed up with political manoeuvrings. They are angry and frustrated, living under rules which are often confusing. This is magnified when focus groups fan the flames of conspiracy which in turn leads to further angst and foreboding on one hand and discrimination and bias on the other. Many are feeling alone and lost.

On a brighter note, having had to shield myself over the years from charges of not having a proper job and actors are just lazy, it has been such a pleasure to see that during lockdown the public have turned to actors, singers, dancers, musicians and all in the arts industry to boost their spirits. We are now 'essential workers'.

It has been intriguing to watch people turn back to 60s and 70s entertainment, with younger audiences on a voyage of discovery and enjoyment, while older audiences enjoy the rediscovery and nostalgia of forgotten favourites.

During lockdown I wrote a TV series, *HELLO LOVELY*, a surreal political satire that taps into the vein of interest for young and old looking for something new. A unique storyline with scenarios everyone empathises with. All situations explored in the project are based on true experiences. They may seem extreme at times but they are, nonetheless, based on truth.

There are many supporting *HELLO LOVELY* including several *Doctor Who* actors. Hopefully, someone will have the courage to pick it up.

Watch this space, as the saying goes. Correct…?

2

Baggage

There has been plenty of time during Lockdown (2020/21) to read through correspondence and notes from fans and others. To analyse and establish exactly how different people cope with what's going on in the World around them.

There are very amusing anecdotes or perhaps I should say, frustrating at the time but rib tickling when recounting them. An example from April Jennings reminded me of a similar experience I had, I'm sure many of you will recognise it too.

April had a doctor's appointment on a Tuesday afternoon. On the Monday she received a txt message, reminding her of the appointment. When she turned up at the surgery as planned, she was told she didn't have an appointment that day. April showed reception the txt she received from them the day before only to be told it 'Isn't in the diary'. Instead of making a fuss April said she would wait until the doctor was available. She was then told the next available appointment was in ten days' time!

Max Cartridge is a large gentleman, like me. One of his anecdotes rang a bell having experienced the same. He was walking along the pavement one day when a young man half his size crossed from the other side of the road and deliberately headed towards Max with his arms stretched wide open. 'Oh, excuse me' said the young man, very loudly so everyone could hear. 'Let me just walk around this round-a-bout in the middle of the pavement'.

The young man proceeded to give Max a wide berth. In doing so he had to step into the road and got knocked down by a motorcycle. He was quite seriously hurt; an ambulance had to be called.

In my case I was in Croydon, South London. Doing my chores for the day, minding my own business when I became aware of yet another young man, crossing from the other side of the road with his arms out wide shouting, 'who ate all the pies then?'. Too busy looking at me he hadn't noticed a Tram, which promptly knocked him down. Fortunately, he wasn't hurt too much, though there was blood coming from his mouth. Unfortunately for me, he got up and charged towards me and knocked me to the ground. He was about to kick nine bells out of me when two Policemen came to my rescue.

Clearly what Max Cartridge and I experienced was blatant, mindless discrimination against large people. What we both came away with from these experiences is, 'what was I doing to be attacked?'. From subsequent correspondence it is clear we both had to cope with various emotions. We were puzzled as to why these youths chose to attack us. There followed a period of anxiety, sudden weeping followed by anger. Having Tony by my side helped me tremendously. I understand fully how difficult this situation would be for someone who lives alone.

This experience has scared me. I've tried to put it behind me but every now and then it comes back to me. The emotional feelings are highlighted by what other people have told me they have experienced. False accusations. Malicious gossip. Chinese whispers.

Ultimately, circumstances like these are going to pray on your mind, distract you and prevent you from functioning. In other words, they become your 'Baggage'.

You need to get rid of your Baggage or at least learn how to put it into perspective and move on.

When I first went to Field End Infants and Junior School in Ruislip, Middlesex, aged 5, I was short and skinny. Add to that I wore National Health tortoise-shell spectacles with a very thick lens for my right eye. As a result, they sat on my face at a slight angle. An obvious target for the bullies. They used to grab my spectacles and deliberately break them. Whilst waiting for new ones the old ones were held together with Sellotape. Giving the bullies yet another reason to thump me. I was targeted because I was the runt of the class, an easy target for the big brave thugs.

As I moved to senior school, I gradually started to gain weight. My eating habits hadn't changed. Although I wasn't sporty in any way, I was active. There was no explanation as to why I ballooned. On my sixteenth birthday I had a medical at school where I weighed 16 stones, 1 lb (225 pounds).

The doctor laughed out loud when I said I didn't eat any more than anyone else. He told me that if I didn't do anything about my size, I would be dead before I was 32. So now, I found myself being bullied because I was big. When it got around that I played the piano and clarinet as well as sing in the school choir the bullies circled. I was the target for both students and teachers.

Despite the frustration of being bullied it never crossed my mind not to go to school. Although it was daily abuse there were joyous times. In fact, taking up music, playing in the school orchestra and band helped me tremendously as did joining the London Borough of Hillingdon Music School. My grandmother was extremely proud when I was appointed the Borough's Principal Bass Clarinet player. When I explained to her that I was the principal player, because the Borough only had the one Bass Clarinet, she immediately came back at me with, '…and you were the one person they chose to give it to'…. 'Oh yes', I thought, 'that's right, there were many other clarinettists, who were better players than me'. What a confidence boost my grandmother's comment gave me!

3

False Accusations

*Some names in this chapter have been changed to preserve anonymity.

Many of you have written to me or chatted online about the anxiety you have when you feel you're being falsely accused of something. In most cases it's not a feeling at all – the accusations are blatantly untrue. They, like all forms of bullying, become *the elephant in the room* and need to be addressed otherwise they'll fester.

Marcus* was about 25 years old at the time of this event. His side of the story is as follows: He had been out with his girlfriend, Rachel*, on the Friday evening, all was fine. Because of work they couldn't meet up on the Saturday but arranged to meet up on the Sunday around 11.00 am.

Before going to bed at 1.00 am the Sunday morning, Marcus texted Rachel, 'Night, we still on for 11.00 am?'

He did not expect an immediate response because it was one o'clock in the morning. When he arose in the morning there had been no reply so, he sent her another text. 'Morning, you okay? See you at 11.00 am'.

Still no reply.

When he got to Rachel's house, he honked his car horn. She looked out of the window and waved. As it was raining, he waited in the car. She didn't materialise. He knocked on her front door, no reply. He called her mobile, but she cut him off.

He went back to his car and sent another text, 'Is everything okay?'

Nothing.

After 90 minutes, he decided to go.

Later that afternoon, the police called at his house. Rachel had reported him for stalking. He was stunned. The police checked his text messages and call log and were satisfied he was not a menace.

Naturally, Marcus was devastated.

About three weeks later, images of Marcus in his car, with 'another girlfriend' in the passenger seat, appeared on social media referring to them as 'two timing rats'. Other images showed him letting the 'other girlfriend' out of the car at the local hospital. It was clear she was heavily pregnant.

Rachel's side of the story was that she had been shown these images and told to dump Marcus. She couldn't believe what she saw but it was obvious the other girl was pregnant and Marcus was very caring towards her, which convinced Rachel what she saw was true.

The truth is even more bizarre. The other girl was Marcus' cousin who had gone into labour early. This was nearly two years before Marcus met Rachel.

Why or how the photos of Marcus with his pregnant cousin were taken is unclear. But the images got into the hands of someone who clearly wanted to cause trouble.

This highlights a serious aspect of human and/or society's nature. There are deranged characters who enjoy upsetting people, causing heartache or simply getting a kick out of creating trouble. The perfect example is those who send out computer viruses. It is some sort of sick fun for them. For the victims it's an irritation at best or an expensive repair bill at worst.

Another character who can make you anxious is the one who enjoys publicly humiliating others. Nothing too serious but enough to upset you and make you wonder why.

Helen* mentioned an occasion when she was at work. She was at the office photocopying machine scanning documents. In addition to her office work, she needed a copy of a passport and driving licence. She scanned them quickly, but mistakenly sent them to a colleague's email address. Instead of discretely letting Helen know what had happened, her colleague stood up and made a public announcement about it; saying it was wrong to use office equipment for private matters, and promptly left the office to report the 'criminal' activity to senior management. Fortunately for Helen, the manager she had to report to was more understanding and the matter was forgotten.

This reminds me of when I was Deputy Theatre Manager at The Broadway Theatre in Barking, Essex.

The open plan office upstairs was busy, everyone focusing on their work. As I walked into the office, Isaac* stood up and announced, 'Simon, you were very lax last night. You left the office windows open before leaving. A very serious security risk.'

Everyone turned and stared at me. Very awkward.

'Not me,' I responded.

'I was the first in this morning,' said Isaac. 'They were wide open. You left them open before locking up last night.'

'Isaac,' I retorted, 'I was not Duty Manager last night. I'd left for the day by 3.00 pm.'

An awkward pause.

Isaac was about to comment when Shelly* stood up. 'Actually, I was the first in this morning, it was me who opened the windows because it was very warm and stuffy.'

Embarrassed, Isaac returned to his desk and tried to disappear.

I was upset and angry but too busy to confront Isaac at that time. On reflection, it was good I was busy because I might have mishandled the situation. An opportunity arose later that day when Isaac and I were alone in the office.

'Have I done anything to annoy or upset you, Isaac?'

'Not at all.'

'So, what was that all about this morning?'

Silence

'I accept your apology,' I said, knowing he hadn't offered one. 'Why was there the need to try and humiliate me?'

Silence

'If you have anything you'd like to talk about, I'll be happy to listen,' I offered. 'But avoid trying the stunt again because all that'll happen is what happened this morning. You'll end up with egg on your face.'

'Are you threatening me?' he snapped.

'Not at all,' I replied. 'What this morning exposed is you know nothing about me, but your actions have told me everything about you.'

'What do you mean?'

Although it felt good getting my own back there was still the issue; why did Isaac want to attack me in the first place?

He tiptoed around me for a few weeks. It's a shame, I rather liked him and he was, in my opinion, good at his job. One thing I observed about him was he could spot a new shirt or a freshly laundered one from a hundred yards. He'd approach guys asking them where they bought their shirts. He could be seen at times, feeling and sniffing the collars and cuffs. In doing so, of course, he had to place his hands on the person wearing the shirt. It was hysterical; he had a shirt fetish.

Addressing the elephant in the room is important, but it also must be managed carefully. Hayley* tells me of her last day at a company she'd worked at for about two years. She worked in an office with seven other people. She enjoyed her work but there was a very bad atmosphere. Literally. There was someone who had very bad odour. Initially, she tried to work out who it was, but it was difficult. She tried to hint at the issue by saying things like, 'Gosh, someone's got a very strong perfume or aftershave.' Didn't work so she brought in flowers with a strong scent as well as air fresheners; purposefully spraying the office so everyone could see what she was doing. Hoping the guilty party would get the message.

On her last day, everyone in the office presented Hayley with a leaving card and a series of gifts. They were all variations on toiletry bags, scented soaps, bubble bath: two carrier bags full. It suddenly dawned on her. They thought she was the stinker. Naturally she was upset but she tried to make a joke of it.

A similar thing happened to me when working at a housing association. Those of you who've read *My Dalek Has A Puncture* will recall Tony, my husband, worked for the same association. You will also recall I was regularly called to the HR Department. Rather like a naughty schoolboy being sent to the Head Teacher.

Tony gave me a call. 'Heads up, HR on the war path.' He ended the call leaving me confused. Was it something in general or was it to do with me personally? Again, I was very busy. I took the view if it was for me, I'd find out soon enough.

A colleague, Barry* approached me. 'You're in big trouble mate'.

I looked on, waiting for an explanation. 'And…?'

Barry put his hands up, eyes wide open and walked away. Naturally, this was de-stabling. WTF? I could feel my heartbeat and a sense of doom.

Two HR officers approached and asked me to follow them. They escorted me to one of the small meeting rooms on the floor. It transpires that there was a very bad smell in the men's toilet along the corridor and it had been reported that I was the one who created it. There followed a very strange conversation where I was informed that two people had entered the men's after I had left and had to leave because the smell was so bad. I was informed HR were concerned about my health and I should seek medical advice.

As you can imagine, I was momentarily dumbstruck. But then I found myself saying, 'I don't use the toilets on this floor, I use the disabled toilets on the floor above.'

Silence.

'Because of my mobility issues, plus my size it's more comfortable. Besides I only wee at work. There's never the need to take a dump!'

As you can imagine, I was somewhat put out. Outraged is too strong a term but I was angry and upset. Why was I accused when it wasn't me? HR mismanaged the issue, too. Why didn't they simply call me to their office as they would normally do … why the public spectacle?

Discrimination.

Obviously, it's the Fat Man who produces Fetid Faeces.

As I left the room, I informed HR they would be hearing from my solicitor. It was an empty gesture spawned by anger and pain. No way was I going to instigate any long, drawn-out proceedings, that would probably fizzle out and end up being expensive.

The following day, I received an email informing me my holiday entitlement had been increased by two days. When I asked colleagues if their holiday entitlement had been increased, No, was the answer. A small chuckle emerged from within. This must be the way HR had chosen to apologise for what happened the day before.

Who was the person responsible for the foul odour in the toilet? No idea. It seems once HR couldn't pin it on the fat guy, they didn't bother looking for anyone else. Apart from the initial embarrassment I soon forgot about it. On the other hand, suspicious colleagues wondered why I got two extra holiday days and they didn't.

When I first started appearing at Sci-Fi conventions and other events, Virginia Hey told me I should be careful about what I say because, 'It could get out that you cannot keep secrets and that would be bad.' At first, I had no idea what she was talking about. A few months later it came to my attention that there were rumours going around that I was to appear in *Game of Thrones* – full story in *My Dalek Has Another Puncture*. Fortunately, I was able to put a stop to the rumours. I've never appeared in *Game of Thrones*. I auditioned but didn't get the role I was up for. I have made it clear on many occasions, and I repeat now, I never mention any job I have done or am doing without the permission of the production company. Even when given permission, I say nothing until I've had sight of, or been given, the official publicity.

One common factor when being falsely accused is you are shouted down; not given an opportunity to defend yourself. From my experience, this is proof your accusers are lying. The way to deal with these is try and keep calm. Make notes, if you've got written proof of an accusation, file them and produce them should things go further. In the main, ignore it. If you are approached about the same accusation again simply say you have no idea what they are talking about and move on. It drives your accusers mad.

4

The Little Things

*Some names in this chapter have been changed to preserve anonymity.

One situation I find interesting is how we allow quite simple and trivial things distract us leading to an increase in stress levels. Suddenly these tiny, ridiculous things lead to something more serious.

Walton's Façade is a wonderful musical piece where a series of nonsense poems by Edith Sitwell are recited over an instrumental accompaniment by William Walton. There are normally two who recite; one male and one female. Many years ago, I was asked to take part in a performance along with a friend of mine, Maggie*.

She was a stunning young lady who was extremely talented. She played the bassoon and sang in choirs and was a joy to watch. We were able to have the poems in front of us on a music stand which was helpful but some of the poems were major tongue-twisters at speed. It really meant, to a certain degree, we had to learn them.

We met a few times together just to go through lines. We also had a run through with the musicians. On the day of the performance, we had a rehearsal in the afternoon and the performance in the evening. Just before the run through in the afternoon Maggie arrived in full performance regalia, wearing a beautiful emerald coloured satin ball gown. My simple dinner jacket and bow tie outfit were still in my car as I decided not to change until the performance.

Maggie went berserk.

She shouted at me in front of everyone saying she had told me to come to the rehearsal in full dress because she'd arranged for photographs to be taken. She hadn't told me. The conversation I recalled was with the event promoter who asked if it was okay for publicity and press photographers to snap away during the evening performance. Besides, the musicians were dressed down too and furthermore, there was no photographer.

There was tension between us during the rehearsal. Maggie felt I had ignored her 'instructions' and I wasn't sure how to deal with her bizarre behaviour. She stormed off afterwards without saying a word. A mutual friend told me not to worry and that Maggie was only nervous for the evening performance.

The event was for charity and our Walton's Façade was at the very end of the second half. Maggie wasn't at the event at the beginning – which she should have been. Nobody could get hold of her and there was concern she wasn't going to turn up at all. There was the suggestion of pulling the Façade. I said, No, I'd cover both parts. So, what was promising to be an enjoyable evening turned into nervous tension and doubt. I found a corner somewhere and focused on familiarising myself with Maggie's text.

It was incredibly stressful. The second half was due to start. Maggie had not arrived. Okay, this is it. I'm going to have to recite the whole thing alone. I could hear a few Doubting Thomases, 'It's ridiculous, he's not rehearsed her part … It's not going to work, he's going to make a fool of us all … It's going to ruin the whole event …' It didn't help the situation but some of the sentiments I felt myself.

It was time. I walked on to the stage as practiced, my heart in my ear, only to find Maggie already in place. I felt awkward because it looked as if I was late. Throughout the performance, in the back of my mind I wondered why Maggie was behaving the way she was.

On a positive note, the performance went well. Compliments all round except from Maggie. She didn't like the outfit I was wearing (usual penguin black tie), I lacked energy which reflected on her. All nonsense of course. I tried to brush it off, but it put a cloud over an event I'd been looking forward to. Furthermore, she refused to stay for photographs: My first experience of working with a diva, I thought.

Joking apart, the experience had a long-lasting effect on me. We parted our ways and I've never seen or spoken to her since. It took a long time to get over it. The main thing buzzing round in my head was, what was Maggie's problem? Had I genuinely upset her, if so in what way and why didn't she discuss it with me? It gradually became a distraction; I couldn't focus on other matters. When I discussed it with my grandparents all they would say was, 'Dwelling on it won't solve anything, try and move on.' Another friend told me I would never find out what was in Maggie's head so chalk it up to experience. There was then a phrase I heard a lot when I was bullied. 'It's all character-building, Simon, character-building.'

A lot of water has flowed under the bridge and looking back; putting things into perspective, it was quite a tiny thing, and I shouldn't have let it upset me. Learning to bite the bullet resolves issues quickly and you can sleep more comfortably.

5

Grief

Andrew Smart

The natural cycle of life inevitably has a sad ending. A birth is an exciting and joyous time. A death is disturbing because of its finality and the realisation that a life is over; you can do nothing about it. We all try to rationalise the loss of a loved one either through faith or comforting ourselves that those who had difficulty towards the end are no longer in pain.

2021 is a significant year for me because I turn 60. Many in the past have told me I wouldn't reach this milestone. I chuckle because they have left this mortal coil years ago. There's a tingle of regret too because I'm unable to stick my tongue out at them.

In May 2021 my good friend Andy Smart died. He was only 57. Those of you who've read *My Dalek Has A Puncture*, the first in this trilogy, will recall me mentioning Andy.

He was a stuntman who doubled for George Clooney and Matt LeBlanc and many others including me. Originally, I said we first met when working on the TV Drama, *The Bill*. Since publication, Andy reminded me that before *The Bill* we met when filming a short film and he was my stunt double. Sadly, I cannot remember the title of the film and it appears to have faded away into the ether.

We both started our adventure in this industry at the same time. His passing has hit me more because of this. He was a probationary stuntman initially and I saw the determination he had to succeed. He was a vegetarian, didn't smoke, drank very little alcohol, kept to a rigorous fitness regime: physically in top form.

It strikes me as particularly cruel; Andy was diagnosed with a very aggressive form of cancer in February 2021 and was dead by May. Mercifully short. But I can't help reflecting on the times he used to rib me about my size and eating habits. Generally, when we managed to go out together for a meal, I'd select a salad or vegetarian option and he would joke, 'Are you telling me you're on a diet?' – No, I often have a salad or vegetarian option as a choice.

My grandmother died in 1988, my grandfather in 1990 and my sister in 1994. Massive rocks in my life gone. The sense of loss even today cannot be expressed easily. What I realise now is I was adrift for about five years. Numb. Rudderless. No real sense of anything. It's only on reflection I feel I must have been living through an emotional breakdown. Fortunately, I was quite busy at the time and didn't think about it or realise it.

I had plenty of acting work and, between engagements, I found it reasonably easy to find temp work. You often hear people say work helps you through a bereavement. At a certain level, I agree.

And there were and are a few good life-long friends who unknowingly helped me a lot.

There are those who read of my exploits traveling from one continent to another and of the work I've been doing and imagine I have a glamourous lifestyle which they envy. At a certain level I agree with them but there is always a Yin & Yang.

The positive is learning about different people and cultures first-hand. Seeing the landscapes from the sky when there is no cloud is breath-taking and makes you appreciate the beauty of Planet Earth. The most fascinating of all is seeing how other countries view the United Kingdom. It's hilarious what they say sometimes.

The downside for me is dealing with authorities both in the UK and abroad when there is clear discrimination on the part of some jobsworth officer, judging me by my country of origin or the hyphen in my name.

On more than one occasion, British Airways has extorted money from me. Fisher-Becker has a hyphen. All correspondence has the hyphen. Occasionally the boarding papers don't have a hyphen and they say the other side (USA or Europe or wherever) won't accept it. The issue? British Airways' system at the airport doesn't allow hyphens. They send me to another desk where I have to get a 'change of name' without the hyphen and they charge me £40.

As you have probably guessed, there is no issue with my hyphen at the other end. But then occasionally, I get to the hotel to find the organisers of an event haven't paid for the rooms and I have to hang around for hours until it is sorted.

As I've said, my grandparents and sister, Pennie, were my rocks. My grandparents sacrificed so much to give us a start in life and Pennie was my biggest fan. When I go on these jollies, as Tony calls them, I think of them and try to enjoy everything they didn't get a chance to. When the likes of BA try to extort money, I hear my grandmother say, 'Just let it go, pay and move on,' and Pennie laughing. These memories of them help me deal with my grief.

6

Pressure Valves

A topic that regularly crosses my desk is stress around family issues. As mentioned in *My Dalek Has A Puncture*, my family has had its share of difficulties over the years. We joke amongst ourselves that there's a family photo by the word 'dysfunctional' in the dictionary.

'Should you be giving advice on family matters, then?' I hear you cry. It's a fair question, to which I respond: when we dug down to the root cause of my 'crises' most of the issues were the result of broken promises from those who claimed they could help, or from interfering busybodies making up stories to fit their theories about my family.

When reading messages from fans or having conversations with others it's clear the same sort of thing is continuing today. Why? What is it that's prevented society from developing an attitude that's more non-judgmental?

When it comes to bringing up a family, there are so many 'experts' with equally as many contradictory ideas, formulae and tactics, that it's no wonder young parents become confused, paranoid and stressed. A position that hits a chord with me is neighbours looking down on a family, making hurtful comments and spreading malicious rumours without taking the time to meet the family and understand what their issues are.

For reasons highlighted in *My Dalek Has A Puncture*, my brother, sister and I were brought up by our grandparents. For us it wasn't a problem. Nowadays, this situation happens a lot more. But in the early 1960s, in the aspiring stockbroker area of South Ruislip, it wasn't the done thing. Add to that the ethnicity of my father. As far as the area was concerned my mother had married a Martian and it shouldn't be allowed.

From my perspective, we benefitted from the experience. Our grandparents had learned a great deal bringing up our mother and aunt. We were their second family where, as my grandfather used to joke, 'We can get things right.' I'm often criticised for being old-fashioned. I accept my work ethic and some values will look that way. My grandmother believed basic psychology should be taught in schools because it would help every family.

We all sat around the same dinner table, ate the same food had the same influences. Yet me, my brother and sister were vastly different people physically, with different personalities, very different talents socially and politically. We were individuals. I say 'were' because Pennie died in 1994 aged 36. We had our sibling rivalries, naturally, but when there were issues, we talked to each other. Not in a family conference necessarily but more on a one-to-one basis. Thanks to our grandparents we learned communication is more important than anything else.

To help others, including family and friends, give the best advice you have to tell the truth and above all be honest with yourself. If it's established you haven't been genuine and sincere, people will begin to distrust you and won't be able to help.

Explaining your crisis can be embarrassing at first. There may be an initial outburst and/or anger from others but once everything is out in the open, you'll feel better and find people will empathise and help.

7

New 13th Sign of the Zodiac

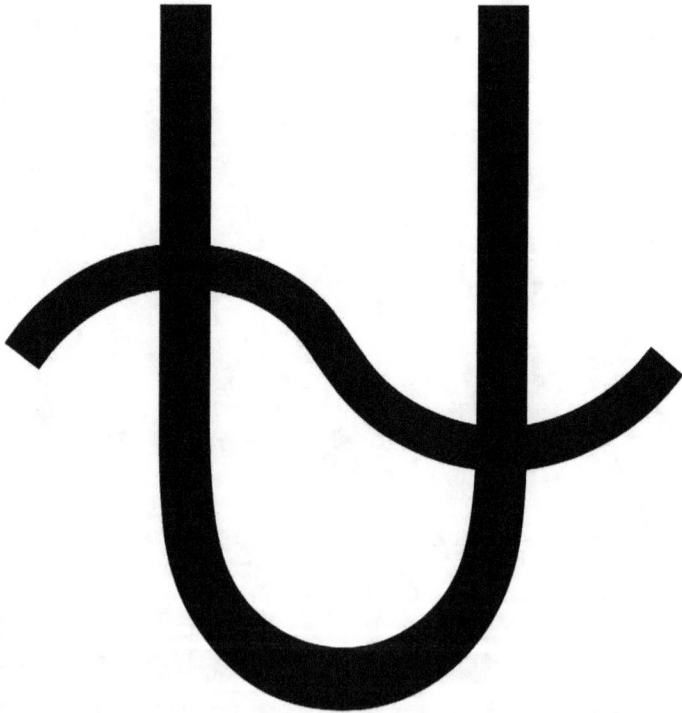

OPHIUCHUS – pronounced: OFF-EE-YOU-CUS.
A new sign of the Zodiac?

Astrology is an interesting topic of conversation. Not to be confused with astronomy which is a fascinating subject of study.

According to the Oxford English Dictionary:

- Astronomy is the study of everything in the Universe beyond the Earth's atmosphere.
- Astrology is a pseudoscience; a type of divination that involves the forecasting of earthly and human events through the observation and interpretation of the fixed stars, the Sun, the Moon, and the planets.

Humans are by nature very curious about what's going on around them. At the same time, we're also frightened and turn to an unknown entity to give us peace of mind and comfort. This is where God and other spiritual beliefs come into play.

In the 14th century the term 'mistike' entered our parlance.

Derived from the Old French 'mistique' meaning mysterious or full of mystery, or directly from the Latin 'mysticus' meaning of secret rites, or the Greek, 'Mystikos' secret, connected with mysteries, MYSTICISM is within us all at certain levels. We all believe in a GOD of some sort or something more spiritual.

Whichever it is, it gives us great calm and understanding of the world. I respect different cultures have different faiths and the stories from all religious texts are fascinating. I'm uncomfortable though when one religious doctrine tries to impose itself on to other faiths. Over the centuries there have been many religious wars which, in my opinion, were and are appalling.

British history is full of such atrocities; Richard the Lion Heart and his crusades, for example, used religion to raise armies and obliterate other parts of the world to gain power and riches.

Religion has been blamed for interfering with scientific development because the scientific facts weakened religious beliefs. Galileo Galilei for example was imprisoned for revealing the Earth moved around the Sun. I enjoy theology but am uncomfortable with religion.

Let's get back to astrology and more importantly the zodiac.

Capricorn	22 December - 19 January
Aquarius	20 January – 18 February
Pisces	19 February – 20 March
Aries	21 March – 19 April
Taurus	20 April – 20 May
Gemini	21 May – 21 June
Cancer	22 June – 22 July
Leo	23 July – 22 August
Virgo	23 August – 22 September
Libra	23 September – 23 October
Scorpio	24 October – 21 November
Sagittarius	22 November – 21 December

This table shows the twelve signs of the zodiac with corresponding dates that have been in place for thousands of years. It is said that for each sign of the zodiac there are certain traits. When we look at ourselves some of us are convinced, we have certain traits for the zodiac sign we are born under.

Take my birthday, 25 November. This makes me a Sagittarian. The symbol is a centaur archer: half man, half horse wielding a crossbow.

When I've read about the positive and negative traits of a Sagittarian I identify with a lot of the suggestions:

On the positive side: optimistic, spontaneous, curious, philosophical and fair-minded, as well as generous, honest, a good orator and conversationalist, idealistic with a great sense of humour.

Yes, this is me.

On the negative side: impatient, direct speaking, lacks tact, finds difficulty accepting criticism, many interests mean master of none, and easily angered.

Must accept I have elements of all these negative traits?

It is said a Sagittarian's favourite colours are orange, red and yellow. My favourite colours are in fact yellow and green. It's difficult for me to confirm one or the other. If coerced I'd plump for yellow. Some would say, for obvious reasons, blue has become my significant colour. I've read somewhere that yellow is positive, green is spiritual. When looking at myself I agree.

Knowing your star sign and establishing if you match any suggested traits is fun but, in my opinion, shouldn't be taken too seriously.

Hand in hand with the zodiac, are horoscopes and astrologists, soothsayers and the like, who interpret what's going on in the world or, for an individual in many cases, try and forecast the future.

The earliest records of the 'reading of horoscopes' go as far back as the Babylonians, 3000 years ago. These are based on several belief systems that say there's a relationship between astronomical phenomena and the personalities of the human world. Astrology relies on fixed celestial points in the night sky. Scientific testing has found no evidence to support these claims mainly because the position of celestial points has changed. Everything in the universe and beyond is constantly on the move.

It is dangerous, in my opinion, for people to read horoscopes and absorb everything without questioning it. Many have written to me to say they haven't done something or travelled somewhere, gone to weddings or birthday parties because they read that the stars were not in the right position or whatever.

Listening to or reading horoscopes increases stress levels. Read them but avoid thinking they are accurate and will improve your life. It could be argued they are another example of something helping you to avoid responsibility for your actions and to stop thinking for yourself.

In recent years, there's been huge publicity about NASA introducing a new 'thirteenth' sign of the zodiac. In truth, a new constellation was discovered, OPHIUCHUS. In a blog it mentioned it could mean there are thirteen Zodiac signs. This was not meant to be a serious suggestion just a hypothesis.

The idea of a thirteenth, fourteenth, fifteenth or higher zodiac sign has been in the ether since the 1930s.

It is only in recent years, however, that new astrological charts have been drawn with each sign allocated different dates. This, or course, has resulted in many of us finding we now fall under a different star sign.

Capricorn	21 January - 16 February
Aquarius	17 February – 11 March
Pisces	12 March – 18 April
Aries	19 April – 13 May
Taurus	14 May – 21 June
Gemini	22 June – 20 July
Cancer	21 July – 10 August
Leo	11 August – 16 September
Virgo	17 September – 30 October
Libra	31 October – 23 November
Scorpio	24 November – 29 November
Ophiuchus	30 November – 17 December

In my case, I'm no longer Sagittarius, I'm now Scorpio. Confusing because for sixty years I've thought of myself as Sagittarian, holding most of the Sagittarian traits.

So now I must look at Scorpio. On the positive side:

Resourceful – I'm more of a theoretical thinker. I can work out simple solutions to problems but cannot always get others to think the same.

Determined – Yes, once I've decided to do something, it's rare for me to change my mind or give up.

Brave – depends on the situation. If a pride of lions were to enter the room, it would be likely to loosen the bowel, but if confronted by bullies or aggressive authority figures I fight my corner.

Ambitious – to a certain degree I can be competitive.

On the Negative side:

Jealous – not really.

Secretive – only where it comes to the Official Secrets Act.

Resentful – not for myself but maybe for others.

Controlling & Manipulative – Quite the opposite.

Stubborn – a family trait. We often laugh that we can be most stubborn when we know we are wrong. Not so much stubborn, now I'm older.

Favourite colours dark purple and black – Absolutely not. As previously stated, my colours are yellow and green.

Favourite foods, spicy – Nope, I'm a korma man.

The conclusion of this exercise is that I don't fit into Scorpio traits but most of the Sagittarian traits tend to fit me comfortably. This begs the question; wouldn't it be better if we could choose a star sign that suits our make up? In addition, do I really have Sagittarian traits, or have I been conditioned into believing I do?

Astrology and horoscopes are fun and interesting but shouldn't be taken seriously.

8

Right of Reply

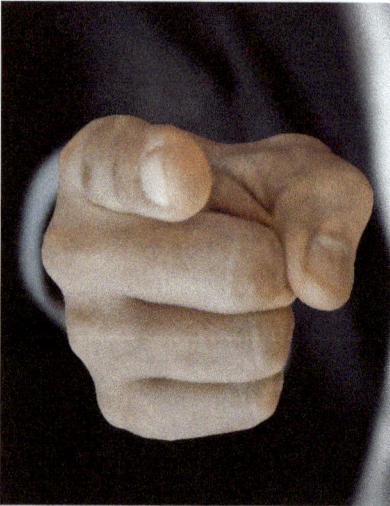

How many times has a finger been pointed at you? Something happens and you're considered the culprit. It's happened to us all. It's extremely uncomfortable and can eat away at you. It can make some people seriously ill.

So many of you have written to me saying how much your lives have been ruined because of rumours, innuendo and blatant lies. *My Dalek Has a Puncture* highlights the bullying I received in my school days. It also mentions a few workplace incidents. All of which instilled an inferiority complex, a sense of worthlessness that killed any sense of ambition and built a lack of distrust in everyone.

Once I plucked up the courage to dip a toe into the entertainment industry I discovered a whole family of like-minded people. The discovery that others had had similar experiences and had what some jokingly refer to as 'luvvie paranoia' was such a release. The damage caused through childhood and young adulthood was deep and irreversible but finding I was not alone gradually helped me come to terms with my past.

Don't get me wrong, the anxiety and fear that prevented me from living life to the full is still there. Deep down. Some might say I'm doing more harm by ignoring and burying things. I argue that there's an element of me saying bugger them all, I'll show them what I can achieve and what worth I can be.

Writing these anecdotes and this chapter in particular is cathartic. In doing so, many of my demons are resurfacing and I confess I'm struggling to get through this. But getting through this I must.

It seems to me that throughout history there have been the bullies and the bullied. Perhaps this stems from a basic instinct. David Attenborough and other naturalists have shown us over the years, monkeys and great apes have a hierarchy that has a degree of bullying. Some in society believe they have power over others who are weaker. This stems from an inbred belief they are superior to others, or it could be some bullies are in fact cowards who can only pick on those who are weaker than them.

Despite finding other actors and entertainers with similar anxieties as myself, learning how it manifests itself can be disturbing and surprisingly opposite to what you'd imagine. The vast majority of people I've worked with are genuinely delightful and a joy to be with. But there is always a bad apple. The answer is to steer clear as far as you can.

As many of you know, I've had the good fortune to work with great actors such as Paul Scofield, Dame Eileen Atkins, Frances de la Tour, Sir Ian McKellen and Sir Derek Jacobi to name a few. All of whom were charming and delightful. I've concluded that this is because they know who they are and are happy with where they are.

Those who are not so happy with their lot can be the difficult ones who, in some cases, take their dissatisfaction out on others. When I first experienced this, I was thrown. Their behaviour was a cloud over the production, turning what began as a wonderful and enjoyable experience into a nightmare. Fortunately, there weren't many such experiences but when they did arise, I found myself asking, 'Who do I need to sleep with to get out here?'

Fortunately, most acting jobs don't last that long, so dealing with awkward situations is tempered by knowing it won't be for too long.

One of my professional joys is green room banter. Not just the gossip. It's the fascinating stories other actors have to tell, especially those older than me. In joining in, I find they've had similar experiences to me. To realise I actually know of some of the actors referred to from years ago (Irene Handl, Joyce Grenfell, Alistair Sim, Robertson Hare et al) is such a buzz especially when it helps me bond with actors I respect.

It's amazing what sort of snippets you pick up. In 2019, the BBC produced *Dad's Army – The Lost Episodes*. Arthur Lowe originally played Captain Mainwaring, and Arnold Ridley played Private Godfrey. In the 2019 series, Kevin McNally played Mainwaring and Timothy West played Godfrey. Here's an interesting fact: Timothy West and Prunella Scales (Sybil from Fawlty Towers) first met and fell in love when working together in a production of *The Ghost Train*, originally written by Arnold Ridley.

Other stories shared include having to tolerate other actors trying to distract you or put you off. Examples include:

Delivering your lines only for the person you're working with to mutter, 'Is that all you're going to give me?' When this first happened to me, luvvie paranoia kicked in. Why did she say that? Was I not doing it right? Oh my God, am I a crap actor? Fortunately, I mentioned it to another cast member who said she'd had the same experience from the same actor. Finding from green room banter that many other actors have had the same experience was true therapy.

Another game, as I call these experiences now, is for an actor to complain I'm too convincing. Being a character actor, I often play people with dubious morals (Dorium Maldovar – perfect example) or who are completely nasty – a bullying father or ugly sister.

One of the earliest productions I was involved in was *Tunnels Without End*, (first mentioned in *My Dalek Has a Puncture*) a play about Tchaikovsky performing at the New End Theatre in Hampstead, London. I played the head of the conservatoire Tchaikovsky attended. In the last act I had a forthright discussion with Tchaikovsky which ended with him storming out of my office. It was a very effective scene and I looked forward to it. The audience appreciated it, but what I didn't realise was the actor playing Tchaikovsky felt I was too realistic, and reported that I was taking the chance to publicly humiliate him. He thought I was attacking him. I must admit my ego glowed in the praise from audience members after each show. I had no idea why it was thought my performance was 'attacking' any other actors.

In 2016/17 I played an ugly sister in *Cinderella*, partnered with the extraordinary Reece Ryan BCA. I love playing an ugly sister but insist that the scene where Cinderella's invitation to the ball is torn up by the sisters, is played absolutely straight. It's so effective when done correctly. This was the first time I performed on stage using my mobility scooter.

When it came to taunting Cinderella, I couldn't get too physical. I could literally drive circles around her but that was about it. So, I left the finger jabbing and 'getting in the face' stuff to Reece – who was brilliant – and I focused on the verbal, vitriolic abuse. It was huge fun, the audience loved it. Unknown to us, Cinderella reported to the producer that Reece and I were unprofessional. She felt I was delivering the vitriol at her personally and not at Cinderella. It soon became clear she was the company snitch.

Matthew Campbell who was my carer during *Cinderella* was dressed up as a duck and did excellent routines which the audience loved. For some reason Cinderella didn't approve of Matt playing the duck. Why, I have no idea. Towards the end of the production our Buttons ended up in hospital with pleurisy. A replacement was found but wasn't available for a couple of days.

Matt was asked to step in at short notice and grabbed the opportunity with both hands and excellent he was. Despite us all encouraging Matt to get through 'the show must go on' situation, Cinderella disapproved and refused to rehearse the dance routines with Matt. All she kept on saying was, 'It's all unprofessional, it's all unprofessional.' Reece mentioned that he and I had done over twenty pantomimes each. When Cinderella was asked how many she had done it turned this was her first. No more needs to be said.

Having mentioned Matthew Campbell, it is time to address a rather disturbing situation in which Matt and I are totally innocent. It's an example of something spiralling out of control due to gossip, spite and cruelty, caused by others who are trying to cover up their own corrupt and deceitful practices. We suffered from trolling on Facebook and Twitter, abusive phone calls and, what hurt the most, silence from people we thought were our friends.

We managed to get legal advice. Free of charge. The first thing we learned was although we were publicly named, we were not allowed publicly to name our accusers. Secondly, although we had a perfectly good case to take to court at the time, their actions were considered a civil matter not a criminal one. This meant we would have to pay upfront a lot of the legal costs; fingers and toes crossed that we would be awarded costs should we win.

McMillan Williams Solicitors Ltd agreed to send out initial salvos to those involved. The accusations stopped immediately. But twelve to fifteen months later they started up again. In addition to the original trolls there were others repeating the gossip, having never met me or Matt and clearly having no understanding of what they were trolling about. The stress was intolerable. It brought on major anxiety and wellbeing issues for Matt, and I admit I had sleepless nights. It became a distraction where we lost a lot of money.

The real frustration was not being allowed to respond to allegations.

This is our RIGHT OF REPLY:

In April 2016, Matt and I were accused of turning up at an event where I was not a guest, with the sole purpose of approaching other guests and handing out business cards.

To remind you, Matt is a booker. He books celebrities into Sci-Fi and other events. He is my booker and is very good at what he does.

I had attended the EMCON event a couple of years before in Nottingham. It was very successful; it was particularly good for me, and I got on very well with the organiser.

In February 2016, there were email exchanges between me and the organiser which were perfectly cordial. It was agreed I would attend the event again, the following year (2017). Absolutely fine.

The event in 2016 had received bad reviews on the Saturday which was surprising knowing how good the event was previously. I suggested to Matt we should go on the Sunday and give moral support. There were several guests attending who were friends and I thought it would be a change to attend as a 'fan' and catch up with those I hadn't seen for some time. Matt's father, Keith, came along too because he was keen to meet Ayshea Brough. We purchased tickets and entered the event.

Initially, all was good. It was a pleasant change to wander around and enjoy an event. As guests we rarely get a chance to chat with each other, the green rooms are staggered and it's not unusual to get to the end of a convention without meeting all the guests. We happened across Sylvester

McCoy and had the usual friendly banter, during which he asked me what I was up to.

Absolutely natural exchanges between actors.

I told him what was going on and mentioned a possible *Doctor Who* cruise towards the end of the year. Sylvester's eyebrows rose and he wanted to know more. As he was busy, he asked me for my contact details, I gave him one of my business cards and we went our separate ways. All rather jolly ... well, that's what I thought.

We were talking to Samantha and David Howe when three burly gentlemen approached me and Matt and told us we were not welcome and had to leave. When I asked why, we were accused of handing out business cards with the sole purpose of poaching clients. Other bookers had asked for us to be removed.

Naturally I cried foul and tried to explain that I only handed one card to Sylvester for reasons stated above; there was a misunderstanding. We were shouted down: They refused to listen 'Because it will only be lies.'

Keith tried to defend us and was man-handled to one side. This of course upset Matt and it all got rather tense.

I was not on my scooter; Matt was pushing me around in a wheelchair. I asked to speak to the organiser, only to be told he wasn't available. With everyone watching, including other organisers it was embarrassing so I agreed to leave. I asked for a refund for our tickets – which we got.

Before leaving I wanted to say goodbye to a few friends, but the three stooges wouldn't allow it. Whatever direction Matt pushed me in, one of them stepped in front stopping us in our tracks.

When I got home, I wrote to the organiser and complained. His response was extraordinary. He admitted he personally hadn't seen any wrongdoing on our part, but it had been reported to him that Matt had been seen handing out business cards and 'upsetting' other guests and agents.

Furthermore, he 'had heard' from other organisers that Matt was causing a lot of trouble at other events too.

Nonsense of course, but it highlighted a change of attitude towards me from the organiser. What on Earth happened between February and April 2016 for such an extreme change. To this day I don't know.

As mentioned in *My Dalek Has Another Puncture* when Matt first started up his booker agency, he ruffled a few feathers because he was very successful. Matt, being young, had the enthusiasm and innocent naivety of youth. Purely by accident he became aware of a small cartel of bookers with questionable business practices: they were charging organisers three times or more for a celebrity than the amount they were offering their client, pocketing the difference plus taking commission from their client's fee. Some would argue that it's not illegal. I would say it's morally wrong, dubious and dishonest.

They instigated a campaign of establishing where Matt and I were attending and then sending emails to the organisers saying we were both untrustworthy, that Matt was going to 'run off' with their money and cause a lot of trouble for their event.

This was followed by them contacting actors warning them not to have anything to do with Matt or me. Fortunately, most of those approached contacted me to establish the facts. Repeating the sequence of events, of course, sounds farfetched. I'm sure some felt what I was telling them was economical with the truth.

Fortunately, or unfortunately; depending on how you see this, Ian McNeice and I were driving with Matt to an event in Hartlepool, UK, when he received a call from the organiser in Hartlepool. She was distraught. She had been 'warned' about Matt and she was checking to see if he was coming to the event. She had been convinced that Matt and I were not going to turn up. Ian was excellent. He gave her reassurances that we were highly professional and confirmed we were all coming and would be arriving together because we were all in the same car.

The following day at the event Ian received yet another call from another booker warning him about Matt. He soon put them right. Afterwards I said to Ian I was pleased he'd received the calls about Matt because it was proof of what we were saying. We were (and still are) victims of a vicious campaign.

What is clear now, is when I handed over my business card, which had both my agent's details as well as Matt's, the cartel present saw this as an act of skulduggery. They interpreted it as such because of their own dubious practices; they totally missed that it was a simple transaction of me passing on my details when asked for.

The cartel had concerns about Matt because he is an effective Booker. They took the opportunity to bludgeon us by exaggerating what happened at EMCON 2016. One of the claims they made was that they saw other guests visibly upset by Matt and I badgering them. This was a blatant lie as only one card was handed over by me and we only had banter with other guests who were friends.

Ian McNeice let many people know about the calls he received and that he was going to be loyal to Matt. Sylvester McCoy let it be known that he was happy for Matt to book for him so hat's off to them.

Doing conventions and other events, although tiring, is extremely enjoyable. It's an opportunity to meet fans, support charities and earn some money too.

Moving on … Charities:

As many of you know, I support various charities ranging from Care in the Community to Conservation of Planet Earth. Sci-Fi conventions have introduced me to so many different causes supporting organisations that don't always get the publicity they deserve.

This is another reason I do as many events as I can.

For years, everything was hunky-dory. After a while though, everything became quite sour, which is a shame.

I was approached by the organiser of Our Disappearing Planet, charity that attended events and also put on its own events; they were well attended. Because of the wonderful cause it was supporting, many celebrities were very happy to attend, including many who were not necessarily known for Sci-Fi. This was an added bonus for me. Not only was I supporting a cause close to my philosophy, but I got to meet other heroes and people I respected. I recall on one occasion sitting in the green room listening to Nicholas Parsons, Christopher Biggins and Julian Glover discussing their pensions. Very enlightening and very funny. Anyway, I mustn't get distracted.

It wasn't long before I got more involved with Our Disappearing Planet and, along with Matt, we had a reasonable relationship with the organiser … so we thought. He even asked me if I would be an ambassador for the charity.

Rumours started to surface that the charity was bogus, money wasn't going where it should, and that the organiser was a crook. It came to light that the organiser had had a business partner, things didn't work out between them; they went their separate ways … these things happen. But then the business partner, Gregor Gillespie, started to imply the celebrities were part of the scam and started name them, including me. He proceeded to troll a number of us on Facebook and made other public announcements.

As far as I'm aware, all celebrities were offered the same arrangement. We all agreed to sign a certain number of photos for the charity and were paid £1 for each photo. If we were asked to sign 100 photos, we would receive £100. The charity would then sell off our signed photos at the going rate, thereby raising more money for the charity.

Everyone was happy with this arrangement. The charity made the equivalent of 70% to 90% of our fee, which was far more than the usual arrangement where we would be offered a smaller discount and would sell merchandise ourselves.

When the organiser was confronted about Gregor Gillespie's stance, it was clear there was a degree of 'he says, she says,' with each accusing the other of the same thing. It wasn't too clear as to what the ructions were really about. I put a stop to Gregor's postings on Facebook by putting up a vlog revealing his messages and asking him to stop naming celebrities 'Whatever problem you have with Our Disappearing Planet, leave us out of it.'

The main response to my vlog was that it was brave to do and a thank you. One or two suggested that what I did was illegal. In my defence, no one in authority has contacted me and Gillespie has stopped trolling.

The offer of becoming an ambassador to the charity was something wonderful: I loved the idea. In an attempt to defend the organiser, I wrote to a number of the animal charities on the website asking them to confirm they had received donations from Our Disappearing Planet. They all came back to say they had no record of receiving donations and had no idea who the organiser was. They also confirmed they received a few donations directly from celebrities saying they had heard about the charity through Our Disappearing Planet.

It was difficult for me to approach the organiser with what I had discovered, but I had to. After all, I was intending to put my name to the cause. As you can imagine he was livid. 'How dare you spy on me and ruin my reputation with ALL these charities.' He then denied he asked me to be an ambassador, said it was something I made up to boost my image and that I had taken advantage of him. When I tried to defend and explain myself, he just shouted me down.

That's right, just like the organiser of EMCON, he shouted me down. What does this tell you?

When I look back at accusations and confrontations over the years, the one thing they have in common is that the accusers never allowed me a right of reply, or to defend myself. Is this because they know they've either got things wrong and are too weak to apologise or was it all a blatant lie and they don't want to give anyone a chance of exposing them?

Now, when similar situations arise, I'm confident they are the problem and I have nothing to worry about. For those who've had the opportunity to read *My Dalek Has A Puncture* and *My Dalek Has Another Puncture*, I'm no longer worried about challenging people when they wrong me. But there's a proper process to go through to get satisfactory results.

Another situation I despise is people wrongly accusing other people of not doing something, just passing on rumours or gossip, which help to muddy the waters. An example, one of the challenges Matt Campbell had to deal with was being accused of not responding to people's emails – something I absolutely know is unlike him. His make up means he has a pathological need to respond to pings, knocks, bells and other noises that accompany emails and tests.

When someone reported this to me, I asked who hadn't received a response from Matt. The accuser immediately stepped back by saying, 'Oh, it's not for me to say.' I played the game of, 'How can Matt check if he doesn't know who's claiming they haven't had a response?' The accuser demurred, to which my response was, 'Then you're lying.'

Taking control of these situations is the only way to resolve them. Having resolved them you have peace of mind and a better sense of wellbeing.

9

Vlogs & Politics

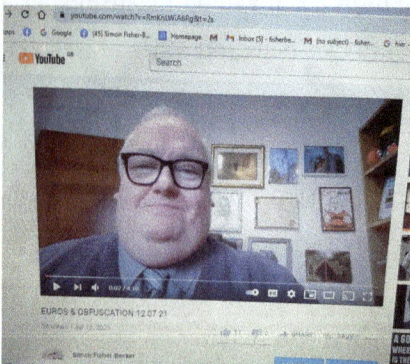

One of the best pieces of advice early on in my acting life was, 'Don't be afraid of getting outside your comfort zone.' Valuable.

Another piece of advice from my sister, Pennie: 'Just take a deep breath and dive in.'

So many opportunities were missed when I was younger because I was too frightened to grab them. Reasons for this are covered in *My Dalek Has A Puncture.*

There are many examples of me feeling awkward or stupid. Mainly because others were telling me I was stupid, thick, a waste of space and I'd amount to nothing. Stage performances before a live audience were wonderful and exciting but occasionally, due to no fault of my own or any other performers, something would go wrong, and I'd feel humiliated. This of course caused my self-confidence to wobble again.

It soon dawned on me though; yes – it was humiliating, yes – I felt stupid and awkward BUT – I didn't die.

From then on, my thought process has been not to harm myself or others, and to allow myself to perform within the constraints of the project. It's the director's job to guide me if I'm overdoing it or not doing enough.

This mind set has helped me tremendously. Theatre helped me build up my stamina. I had the good fortune to work with and learn from the best. My most favourite aspect of theatre work is rehearsals. The opportunity to work in a team to craft a piece of work can only be appreciated by those who have done it.

Then TV and film came along. The first challenge was filming out of sequence. Learning to see where the scene you're doing fits on the arc of the story is not always easy. It's the job of the director to explain where in the story the scene is, the atmosphere, and above all the motivation. I've been lucky so far. I seem to have a built-in instinct, but I worry sometimes that the instinct might have a day off.

The most uncomfortable development was seeing the time for rehearsal being cut back, sometimes to nothing. There would be a few technical runs but rarely any for the actors. Particularly in TV and especially when working on soaps. When I first experienced this, it is fair to say my self-confidence more than wobbled. At the end of the day, I found myself shaking. Over time, I've got used to it, mainly because I started to expect it. The answer? Be prepared. Concentrate on learning the lines, do your own analysis of the scenes and above all concentrate on how you should perform the scenes. Don't be too rigid, allow for input from others, should it come along.

In the main, do your own thing and wait to be asked to provide alternatives. What I've found is my instinctive offerings either hit the nail on the head or I give a slightly different angle that wasn't considered but they prefer it. This was most certainly jumping in at the deep end. Extremely exciting, but over all too soon.

Since *Doctor Who*, what has come my way are opportunities using personal technology. Websites, SKYPE, Zoom, Facebook and many other platforms. The idea of having a YouTube channel and doing Vlogs filled me with dread.

But circumstances forced me to reconsider my position. It is wonderful receiving messages from across the world. I'm staggered that people in China, Turkey, Uzbekistan, Kazakhstan and Mongolia want to contact me. The power of *Doctor Who* and Harry Potter. The brilliance of today's technology bringing us all closer together.

I try to respond to every piece of fan mail I get in the post personally and of course messages that come in via Facebook and Twitter. At times it can be overwhelming and time consuming. Fan mail in the post is always welcome, but it came to a point with electronic communication I found fans were asking the same questions or variations on a theme. This was when I decided to face my dread of doing Vlogs head on.

The dread was initially based on the fear of technology. But I shouldn't have been concerned because once I'd done my research, it turned out, in the main, to be straightforward and not as complicated as I thought. There was plenty of material. Answering questions about Harry Potter and *Doctor Who* or anything to do with the entertainment industry wasn't a problem but then I found I was being asked about other issues of the day. Initially this was tricky.

Questions covering a wide range of topics including, history, theology, science, health, economics and – deep breath – politics. Dangerous territory. At this point I have a confession. As a freelance professional there have been times where I have had to accept temp work between acting engagements. Some of these jobs asked for vocational qualifications – first aid, human resources (personnel), personal license. In the UK, you must sit an exam and gain what is called a personal license if you hold a position where you are a duty manager / officer in a building or marquee where alcohol is sold.

Add to this my academic qualifications, my natural interest in all sorts of topics and that I'll be 60 in November 2021, I have a broad understanding of people and how they cope with life's issues.

Because of this I'm confident I can offer educated opinions – emphasise *opinions* – on a wide range of subjects. As with giving advice, I never tell people what should happen, or what they should do.

Initially my Vlogs were simple and non-complicated and lasted five to six mins. They were fun to do but I didn't want them to take up too much of my time.

Selecting questions wasn't difficult. Likewise mulling them over in my head wasn't distracting. Jotting down notes takes only a few minutes and then recording is purely Press Record-Speak-Press Stop. In addition, I didn't spend time editing, so the Vlogs became a one-take exercise. Once complete I uploaded them on to my YouTube channel and sent links to Facebook, Twitter and by email. The whole process takes about 40 minutes.

My style has become more relaxed, fans seem to like it. In the main I get positive feedback. Some feel at times I can be too political, or my choice of words can be offensive. In my defence, I only make notes; there's no script. Admittedly, there's a degree of extemporisation which can lead to choosing words and phrases that come to mind that could have multiple interpretations.

That said, a major development which never crossed my mind were two radio podcasts asking me to produce 'Simon Says' segments for their shows.

- Joseph McGrail-Bateup from *The No-Name Trivia Show* based in Australia: www.facebook.com/groups/227909668481897 and
- Christian Basel from *The Legend of the Traveling Tardis* based in Florida USA. www.youtube.com/channel/UCL_f2VXUL3ZnKn78gRrdTAA

The No-Name Trivia Show has special guests and I became a co-host. Each show is governed by the 'Letter of the week'.

There is a section called, 'Simon Says' where I talk about a few subjects and select collective nouns beginning with the letter of the week. For example, when it came to the letter 'E', I mentioned vitamin E and the best food sources for it, followed by a brief explanation of existentialism and the wonderful Eartha Kitt. Finally, the collective nouns were: exaltation of larks, embarrassment of riches, bed of eels and a flock of emus.

For *The Legend of the Traveling Tardis*, I provided 'Simon Says Sci-Fi'.

The slant here is towards Sci-Fi elements or themes. Topics covered include: Peter Cushing: who could have been the replacement to Peter Cushing had he regenerated; What exactly is Sci-Fi? Fact or Sci-Fi – are we living Sci-Fi today? Astrology & horoscopes; and What is Voyager telling us?

Each of these spin-off Vlogs has a following and I'm truly grateful to Christian Basel and Joseph McGrail-Bateup for these opportunities. Another spin-off from *The No-Name Trivia Show* came about because one of the sponsors was Highland Titles Ltd. As a result, Joseph and I and another co-host, Paul Boultwood, own a plot of land in Scotland and hold Celtic titles. As mentioned in *My Dalek Has A Puncture*, I already hold a courtesy title Viscount of William and Mona. In 2020, I was gifted Lord Fisher-Becker of the Principality of Sealand and now I'm also Lord Fisher-Becker of Glencoe.

POLITICS

One of the traps my Vlogs helped me fall into was allowing people to think they knew what my politics are. As a result, they've tried to pigeonhole me which has been very difficult. Even at 60 years old I have difficulty fitting into any category. Round-peg-square-hole syndrome pretty much sums up my experience in life.

At school, I studied economics and history which led to a natural interest in politics. As a civil servant in Westminster my experiences gave me the opportunity to witness the political manoeuvrings of the day. Today, it could be said I enjoy armchair politics. There's nothing better than an earnest political discussion particularly when panels are made up of representatives from all parties. The BBC are often criticised for being biased – a cry from every party that's in power, but this is unjust.

The BBC covers Prime Minister's questions live, which admittedly can come over as a childish bun-fight and in my view can tarnish the good work parliament does. The BBC also broadcast government at committee stages and dispatches from the House of Lords. If more people gave a little time to some of these programmes, they would have a better understanding of how British politics works, and learn from experts in their field.

What are my views?

Speaking from the UK perspective, knowing those from outside our shores will concede a similarity with their governments: politicians are a necessary evil. Let's not tarnish everyone because of a few bad apples.

There are some very fine unsung members of parliament who work hard and do an excellent job. There are many backbenchers who work tirelessly without complaint or real recognition for decades.

Partisan politics in my view is flawed and outdated. It creates tribalism and prevents sensible actions and decisions because they clash with an ideology. It can also produce policies that only benefit a few individuals. For these reasons I consider myself one of the growing number of people who support coalitions and independent candidates.

There are times when a national crisis requires a coalition.

In 2007/8 there was a global economic crisis. In the UK, the Labour Government was criticised for 'bailing out the banks' because many believed the financial markets created the crisis in the first place.

The general election of 2010 had a higher-than-expected turnout of nearly 70%. There was no overall control for any party, so the Conservatives went into a coalition with the Liberal Democrats. The consensus is this coalition was effective and Britain weathered the financial crisis well. That is, when other countries including, Spain, Greece and the Republic of Ireland were near bankruptcy, the United Kingdom 'seemed to get through it'. Within five years, finances although not perfect were in a stronger position. Domestically fundamental social issues had been addressed, including the introduction of same-sex marriages.

Another global disaster (COVID) began in 2020. In my opinion this is an example where we need a period of national government akin to the one we had during the Great Depression of the 1930s. The cabinet should be made up of representatives from *all* parties focusing on helping the whole nation and establishing sensible, clear solutions. To be honest, I've been promoting this idea for years and I've been dismissed as being, naïve, ridiculous and a simpleton.

But these comments tend to come from those who are uncomfortable with others who can't be easily compartmentalised. They rarely think for themselves and are frequently hypnotised by a soundbite.

So, am I left wing or right wing?

Does having a social conscience and defending the right of free speech make me a socialist, communist or Marxist? Of course not.

Does the fact I acknowledge market forces, understand the need for law & order, and support an environment to encourage business make me a capitalist or fascist? Of course not.

My grandparents instilled in me the notion, if you are unable to convince, compromise. When I was about 14 years old, I recall my sister telling me that American President Lincoln once said, 'You can please some of the people all the time. You can please all the people some of the time. But you can't please all the people all of the time.'

Two very strong political statements but not necessarily left or right wing. I have firm views across the political spectrum and think of myself as an independent. Most political systems worldwide have what is referred to as an Upper House or Chamber. In the UK, we have the House of Lords. Many argue the House of Lords is undemocratic because it's unelected. I disagree. These arguments tend to be led by those who deliberately avoid the purpose of the House of Lords and accepted by those who allow themselves to be mesmerised by one-liners and slogans.

As a valuable scrutinising chamber, the House of Lords is more democratic than the House of Commons; in addition to partisan benches there are the crossbenches: Peers who aren't affiliated to any party and are free to talk and vote on any topic as their conscience fits. If I were to sit in the House of Lords, I'd be a Crossbencher.

In recent years there has been a lot of talk about mental health and wellbeing. This has been an issue for many years, some would say centuries, so it is good it is being addressed now.

Having lived with family members, known friends with mental health issues and talked to others about their anxieties, their common cry is that problems stem from the difficulty of facing life's trials and tribulations. Some of these can appear to be trivial but most are complex and serious.

There are more and more promotions about being kind to each other, understanding and being supportive of those who need help. This should be a natural instinct. Look at what happens when there is a natural disaster – everyone comes out to help each other. Everyone gets together when there's a terrorist atrocity or an individual goes berserk with and gun or knife or machete. This is when we not only see the compassion of people but witness some true heroism.

Pressures of life can trigger an episode. It could be not being able to pay a utility bill or when applying for help, people find they don't fit easily into categories. More seriously things can turn out to be far more complicated and frustrating, triggering a deeper downward spiral.

This is where the finger must be firmly pointed at the government or other authorities. In my opinion, if a rule or law is overly complicated by too many exceptions then it is a bad rule or law. We've all heard commercials on radio or television where there is a voice over speaking very quickly highlighting side effects or whatever. So fast you can't hear what's said. In those circumstances I don't purchase the product because their advertising gives me the impression their product is flawed.

During the COVID lockdowns in the UK, many rules were introduced. They had too many exceptions and some rules even contradicted other rules. It became a joke, but to some it simply added to their anxiety. The government offered furloughs and other support schemes to help people financially, but millions didn't qualify for a variety of reasons.

Was this unfortunate or were the rules so designed? If the latter then it makes the government's offer of help rather cynical, which again increases anxiety levels.

We've all, at times, complained about our plight; the stresses and strains thrust upon us. The frustrations are compounded because it's not always simple or straightforward to resolve issues. There are ombudsmen and other administrators who can look at complaints, but they have no legal bite. I believe if these bodies were given proper teeth, certain companies, conglomerates, councils and the government itself would reconsider their positions.

The main frustration for most people is money. In recent years in the UK there has been a lot of restructuring within companies; a necessary process for some and an exercise for others. The element that upsets most employees is having to re-apply for their job which in their mind they are doing perfectly well.

With my HR head on, I can see restructuring can be positive. It allows companies to review their working practices and establish what reforms may be necessary, especially with the advancement of technology and more and more companies merging. The negative side I've witnessed is that older members of staff are more likely to be encouraged to take voluntary redundancy, which is, in my opinion – NUTS. Look at the experience and expertise being discarded. A mistake in the long term.

Despite legislation such as the Equality Act there is still blatant discrimination, particularly against the disabled and those with, shall we say, a higher-than-average BMI. Over the years I've been made redundant several times. Because acting is my focus it didn't bother me too much. It still hurts, but for me the redundancy pay-out was more of a cash injection than a loss of a job. The last job where this happened, it was noticeable that of the 60 people made redundant 48 of them were over 45 years old, disabled or had other underlying issues. Sleepless nights and increased anxiety!

For the self-employed, cash flow is a major issue. Many of you have contacted me to express your despair in trying to get paid for work done. Having been self-employed since 1984 I understand fully. It is easier today because most transactions are done electronically; once you receive a payment notice you can check your bank account and find the payment has landed. Yesteryear, we had the 'Cheque's in the post' saga. I recall seeing a cartoon image of the solar system showing the planets orbiting the sun and after Pluto there was 'Cheque in the post'.

To me Occam's Razor has the simple answer to ease cash flow.

Simply legislate that *all* invoices should be settled within six weeks. With today's technology payments can be made easily. There may be a slight hiatus when the legislation is introduced but it'll soon settle down. The self-employed and companies will find it easier to plan ahead knowing finances will be in place. This in turn will help the general economy work and grow.

Politics and economics tend to go hand in hand; each affects the other. Various governments in the UK have introduced legislation to tackle gambling: It destroys so many lives, and yet our entire fiscal situation is no more than sophisticated gambling. When you hear the phrase, 'The markets are buoyant or jittery', it means they've either had a good day gambling on the stock markets or they've made a loss.

Likewise, there is a lot of talk about creating peace and harmony in the world, yet our economy relies heavily on the sale of arms. You will recall the 'weapons of mass destruction' during the days of British Prime Minister, Tony Blair. Was the reason Tony Blair was so adamant the Iraqi President Saddam Hussein had weapons of mass destruction because the British Government sold them to him? If so, this begs the question, if Saddam Hussein didn't have them – where are they now?

There are many people who don't agree with the voluntary sector.

My mother-in-law was such a person. I recall a conversation with her where she said she couldn't understand why people would offer to work without being paid for it. When I told her our whole economy would collapse without volunteers, she laughed at me and dismissed me as a fool. Nonetheless, my statement stands. The capitalist system cannot work without volunteers.

Whatever your political views are, take note; none of it matters if Planet Earth and society isn't safe. By safe I mean we should focus on keeping the environment clean. I've already mentioned cleaning up nuclear waste and producing an abundance of cheap energy, but there should also be public programmes in place to build better sea defences, land reclamation, clearing and dredging rivers and other waterways, and above all repairing and updating our sewage systems.

So much of the UK's waste systems were built by the Victorians. They cannot cope with the excessive amount of waste produced today. We joke about giant fat burgers, but they are real. The infrastructure is collapsing and needs urgent attention. To those who cry, 'Too expensive,' tell me, what will be the cost if we don't act? The serious danger is disease and pestilence and the return of the plagues and pandemics of centuries ago.

I must stop talking politics. From what I've mentioned in previous chapters I think my position is clear. Or to some maybe not.

Dune, the 1965 science-fiction novel by Frank Herbert, mentions Planetologists. These are ecologists who study the ecosystems of entire planets. I'm not claiming to be a planetologist, but I support any programmes that look after the planet, clean the environment and above all build our society into something non-judgmental, creating a better way of life for the 21st century.

The End

A Few Thank Yous

Dan Grubb, Fantastic
Books Publishing

Kim Barry, Agent

Paddy Gormley

Time to acknowledge those who have helped me tremendously to navigate this organic, rocky, mysterious, treacherous yet wonderful, exciting and satisfying vocation.

Thank you Dan Grubb & Fantastic Books Publishing for coming along to a performance of *My Dalek Has A Puncture* one wet Wednesday evening, then offering me a contract to put my show into book form. Thank you again for subsequently commissioning, *My Dalek Has Another Puncture & Let Zygons Be Zygons*. Though a cathartic experience, it proved to me I can write, which helped me through lockdowns tremendously.

Thank you, Kim Barry, for having faith in me when you took over the Jaffrey Management Agency when I was in a vulnerable place after a vicious attack, and for your continued support since 2009. Above all, thank you for getting me the audition for *Doctor Who* which changed my life so much and ultimately led to so many other opportunities.

Thank you Paddy Gormley for writing, *Hamlet: Tragedy of a Fat Man*, a one-man play that stretched me beyond my wildest dreams. The experience built my confidence, made me a better actor and above all a better person and human being.

L to R: Frazer Hines, Gill Selwyn, Matt Campbell

Thank you to all the celebrities who welcomed me on to the Sci-Fi circuit. In this picture we see Frazer Hines who is a representative for everyone. As a fan of *Doctor Who* I remember seeing Frazer as Jamie McCrimmon with Patrick Troughton so it's particularly special we are now good friends.

Naturally, there's a huge thank you to Matt Campbell. His energy in helping me get into conventions helped me travel the world and gain such wonderful experiences. He also arranged book tours which in turn helped with the success of my books. Like me, his grandparents meant a lot to Matthew and when they died recently, he incorporated their surname into his. He is now Matthew Campbell-Dell. There were raised eyebrows when he first announced this, but I support his decision fully. He was also a tremendous help when Tony and I moved house in 2018. Never forgotten.

Thank you to Gill Selwyn, (centre of this picture), who has been such a valuable help to Matt and M&M Famous Faces, particularly at Conventions. Her calming influence and sense of humour has been a joy. She's well-read so conversations cover a broad spectrum away from the entertainment Industry. I'm so pleased we are close friends.

Pantomime was the very first piece of theatre I was taken to when I was about four years old. It was always an ambition to be an ugly sister in Cinderella. It is a definite double act and doesn't work if the team doesn't gel.

A huge thank you has to go out to two highly professional fellow Uglies, Dudley Rogers and Reece Ryan. In both cases we bonded immediately and found it very easy to work together. I first met Dudley in 2001 in Grimsby. He taught me so much about timing and more importantly energy. I first met Reece in 2016 in Manchester. It was the first time I did Panto on my mobility scooter. Reece immediately spotted the comic potential with the positive attitude of 'Where there's a

Dudley Rogers

Reece Ryan BCA

will there's a way'. Above all, we're both accomplished improvisers which is so useful when the unexpected occurs on stage during a performance. Both are now great friends.

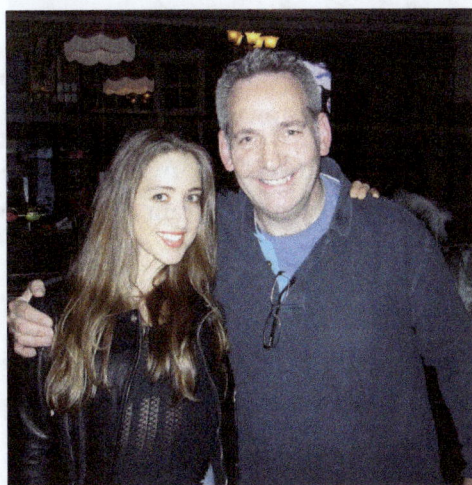

Paul Welch – Photographer

Thank you to Paul Welch, the photographer who helped build my first portfolio. On more than one occasion his photo alone secured me a job. I firmly believe without Paul I wouldn't have had so many opportunities when I first started in the industry.

Scott Radburn   *Joseph McGrail-Bateup*   *Paul Boultwood*

Thank you to Scott Radburn, Joseph McGrail-Bateup and Paul Boultwood from Australia. To relieve the boredom of lockdown the *Joe & Scott Trivia Show* was born in March 2020. It was a radio podcast that had various segments including, 'A Little Bit of Boultee' by Paul Boultwood. I was invited on as a guest from *Doctor Who*. It was huge fun, a mixture of guest chat blended with trivia quiz.

Due to other commitments, Scott had to leave the show and Joe invited me to be a co-host along with Paul Boultwood. The show is now called *The No-Name Show* and is broadcast across the globe.

To expand on what I've said in the previous chapter, in practice Paul and I are co-hosts on alternate weeks and occasionally we are both on at the same time. I introduced my own segment 'Simon Says' where I talk for about three minutes on topics beginning with a certain letter of the alphabet or a number of the week.

Paul's 'Little Bit of Boultee' is always interesting, delivered in a humorous way and is of a very high standard, which of course encourages me to raise my bar. In all the weeks I've been involved with *The No-Name Trivia Show*, Paul Boultwood and I only once mentioned the same topic – but talked about it from different angles. Some suggest we're rivals –

absolutely not. We have contrasting styles which complement each other beautifully.

Christian Basel

Steve Long

Thank you to Christian Basel at *The Legend of the Traveling Tardis*. Christian had come to my table several times when I was at conventions in America and would take selfies holding a miniature Tardis. He joined a number of us at a visit to the Kennedy Space Center, Cape Canaveral, organised by the wonderful Howard Hayes. Christian talked about his show, which was in its infancy at that time. He invited me on as a guest panellist.

The Legend of the Traveling Tardis has grown into a much larger and popular show. It started out as a *Doctor Who* fandom project but now has a much broader remit with a strong Sci-Fi element. Having viewed my personal Vlogs and seen Simon Says on *The No-Name Trivia Show* Christian asked me to do similar Vlogs for *The Legend of the Traveling Tardis*. This is how 'Simon Says Sci-Fi' came along. A wonderful challenge and I can't thank Christian enough.

Thank you to Steve Long for visiting me at 'Potterverse' a Harry Potter Convention in Baltimore, Maryland in 2018. He told me about his spoof audio Sci-Fi-detective series called *The Hawk Chronicles – The Adventures of Kate Hawk* (www.hawkchronicles.com) and invited me to record one episode (no 103) as a guest artiste, playing an MI6 Agent called Tony Simon. I'm very pleased I accepted the offer. It has been great fun and when Steve asked if I knew anyone who would like to join the cast, I introduced Clive Ward and Thomas Ward. Having agreed to do the one episode, Tony Simon has become a regular character appearing in over 80 episodes by the time *Zygons* is published.

Like the 'Simon Says' and 'Simon Says Sci-Fi' Vlogs, *The Hawk Chronicles* have helped me hone my craft and keep cabin fever at bay.

Thomas & Clive Ward

Mark Longman & Jayne McMahon

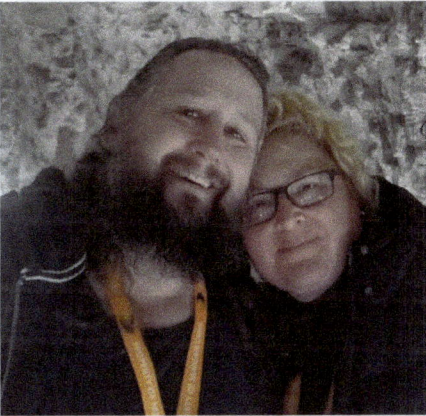

Grant & Eva Perkins

A special thank you to Mark Longman who was an excellent events organiser. His conventions under the banner 'Geeks' were always such fun, well organised and satisfying. Along with his fiancée, Jayne McMahon I was invited to many of his events and discovered vast regions of the UK. Alas, we lost Mark to Covid at the beginning of the pandemic crisis in 2020. Very sad loss. He was such a funny and generous gentleman as well as an honourable gentle man.

Thank you to Grant & Eva Perkins. It is always lovely meeting up with celebrity guests but there are also lesser-known people like Grant & Eva. Grant is an artist and cartoonist who, by his own admission, is a real fan of Dorium Maldovar in *Doctor Who*. Amongst many talents, Eva designs beautiful jewellery. We've often met for dinner when at weekend events, chewed the cud and had a good laugh. Above all Grant's cartoon strips and other 'Dorium' designs have helped keep Dorium Maldovar and me in the fans' minds.

Dorium Mug

Dorium Pillow

Eva's jewellery

And Finally

Tony and Simon

By the time this volume is published, Tony and I will have been together for 30 years. A very long time, people say, but the time has flashed by. What's the secret of a long-term relationship? The true answer is I don't really know.

Putting together this trilogy of autobiographical anecdotes has been cathartic to say the least. The purging of memories has been traumatic on one level but joyous on another. Tony has supported and helped me through this period, as he has for the years we've been together. All occupations have their difficulties both personal and professional. Those who are freelance will understand and appreciate there are certain pressures of work that do not occur to those who are employed. In the entertainment industry this is tempered by actors in particular not having full control of their work.

Having had a brush or dalliance with the music industry when he was younger, Tony fully understands what I have to deal with as an actor.

Over the years he has helped me develop coping mechanisms when luvvie paranoia kicks in or how to control things when I need to rant.

He brings me down to Earth when I get overexcited about anything. When I heard the term 'soulmate' when I was younger, I used to dismiss it but now I understand it more. Tony and I are one unit supporting each other. We have a lot in common but see things from the opposite ends of the spectrum. We also lead separates lives connected by a common interest. Is this the definition of soulmates? I don't know, but I'll take it for now.

It could be said an actor's life is a selfish one. When I first set out, my main focus was to build a CV and a reputation. I was originally told I wouldn't be taken seriously until I was 40. This is why I accepted any job that was offered. It meant I was away from home a lot but in doing so, I built a broad experience across the whole spectrum of the industry from Shakespeare to Panto, film, TV and theatre. Tony understood and still understands this. He did start putting 'You dare!' days in the diary which meant I *had* to be available to do something together on particular dates. In practice it didn't work because I had an inbuilt, work's work and work is money. Added to this was, and still is, the worry of having no idea where or when the next job will come along.

The lockdowns of 2020/21 had a silver lining. Because we couldn't go anywhere or meet anyone, we were together for the longest period of time since 1991. We both have our individual man caves. He his music room and me my office where I concentrated on my writing. By chance I've been offered more audio work including from Big Finish who agreed Tony's music studio was professional enough for them.

Again, Tony is supporting me with whatever comes along, enabling me to achieve so much. We both support each other. This is why I love him and am so pleased to have found him in the world, and why *Let Zygons Be Zygons* is dedicated to Tony.

A thank you to my brother, Erol and my mother, Carole. In our early years, Carole shared the slings and arrows thrown at Erol and me. She was a strong woman and, along with our grandparents, tried to laugh off the nonsense we had to deal with. When our grandparents fell ill, the three of us helped to care for them at home. There was very little help from outside the family – we somehow didn't fit the boxes. We fell into a routine, and all was good, though at times exhausting. But we managed.

Now, Carole is over eighty. Mentally alert but physically frail and Erol is her main carer. I've helped financially when I can, but when my entire income stream came to a full stop in March 2020 it wasn't so easy. Not being able to visit them added to my emotions and frustrations but video

My brother, Erol

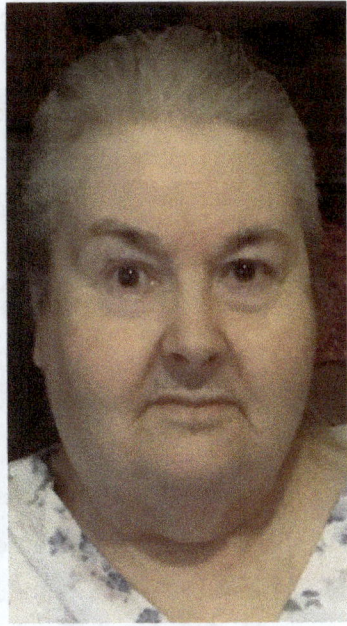

My mother, Carole

SGC 2007-2018

calls have helped, and me calling them has become part of their routine.

Over the years, we had many pets, cats, dogs, gerbils, rabbits. Now Carole and Erol have no pets and feel something is missing. Tony and I haven't had a pet since we lost our cat, SGC, in 2018. SGC for Small Ginger Cat. Not having SGC around has left a hole. Those who've never had a pet will never understand the grief of losing one. To those who have experienced it, I throw you a virtual hug.

To the fans and others who follow me: You are amazing and are the ones who have at times overwhelmed me but also helped me through periods of doubt, when my self-confidence has been bashed.

Thank you so much. Receiving messages via social media or fan mail through the post is truly fantastic, humbling and wonderful.

For those who provide stamped addressed envelopes thank you. A word of caution for those who enclose universal postage coupons.

On the back it clearly states the coupon is 'exchangeable in any country of the universal postal union for the minimum postage for an unregistered

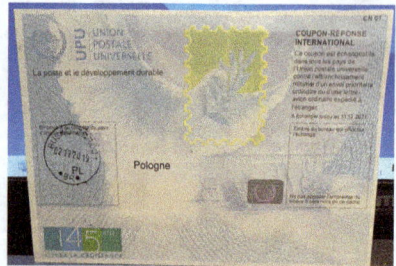

priority item or an unregistered letter sent by air to any foreign country', but sadly in the UK, I've found the Post Office don't accept them. The Post Office agrees the UK is part of the Universal Postal Union – the problem is they haven't the facilities to accept them!

Hopefully my anecdotal ramblings have been interesting and helpful and *Let Zygons Be Zygons* has proved a suitable conclusion to the trilogy.

Remember:
- If you can't convince others, compromise.
- Never leave to tomorrow what you can get done today.
- A stitch in time saves nine.
- Something becomes urgent when it hasn't been properly prioritised.
- If you don't like the way things are, change them. If you can't change them, put up with them.
- Do unto others as you would have them do unto you.
- Find the silver lining.

About the author

A versatile character actor, Simon Fisher-Becker's work has covered a wide spectrum, from Shakespeare to pantomime, film, television, radio and theatre.

He was born at Paddington General Hospital and raised by his grandparents in Ruislip. He left school after A-levels and joined the Civil Service, while taking a degree in Business Administration. He then attended drama college. Denholm Elliott was his mentor.

He was a committee member of Actors and Writers London, previously Hammersmith Actors and Writers Group, of which he was chair from 2000 to 2004. He co-founded the Tilt-Yard Theatre Company which presented new writing and adaptations of established classics.

In March 2009, Simon was a victim of violent crime. He was attacked at a petrol station by a gang and beaten badly, leaving him with permanent damage to his spine and knee. The attack meant that he was still recovering from his injuries in December 2009 and therefore unable to appear in Panto. As a result, he was available for the casting to play Dorium Maldovar in *Doctor Who*.

Between 2013 and 2014 he collaborated with Benjamin Maio Mackay and the Preachrs Podcast. In 2014 he voiced Dorium Maldovar in Benjamin's touring comedy show *50 Years of Doctor Who: Preachrs Podcast Live 2!* which played Adelaide Fringe and Melbourne International Comedy Festival to great acclaim.

In 2014, Fisher-Becker joined Joanna Scanlan and Vicki Pepperdine in the comedy *Puppy Love* for the BBC.

In 2018 Simon joined the International cast of Hawk Chronicles, the

About the author

adventures of Kate Hawk. An audio science fiction drama found on Spreaker, iTunes, iHeartradio – mixcloud.com/discover/kate-hawk.

You can subscribe to Simon's vlogs at: bit.ly/SubToSimonFisherBecker

If you have enjoyed this book, please consider leaving a review for Simon to let him know what you thought of his work.

You can read about Simon on his author page on the Fantastic Books Store. While you're there, why not browse our other delightful tales and wonderfully woven prose?

www.fantasticbooksstore.com

Also by Simon Fisher-Becker published
by Fantastic Books Publishing

My Dalek has a Puncture – getbook.at/FlatDalek
My Dalek has Another Puncture – getbook.at/AnotherFlatDalek